P9-CJL-117

OLYMPIC GOLD 1936

HOW THE IMAGE OF JESSE OWENS CRUSHED HITLER'S EVIL MYTH

by Michael Burgan

Content Adviser: Dennis Showalter, PhD
Professor of History
Colorado College

COMPASS POINT BOOKS
a capstone imprint

Compass Point Books are published by Capstone,
1710 Roe Crest Drive, North Mankato, Minnesota 56003
www.mycapstone.com

Editor: Catherine Neitge
Designers: Tracy Davies McCabe and Catherine Neitge
Media Researcher: Eric Gohl
Library Consultant: Kathleen Baxter
Production Specialist: Laura Manthe

Image Credits
AP Photo: 21, 46, 48, 58 (top), Kurt Strumpf, 58 (bottom), Matt Dunham, 51; Getty
Images: Bettmann, 15, 17, 26, 29, 57 (top), New York Times Co., 18, Past Pix, 10,
33, Print Collector, 59, Stringer/Keystone, 37, ullstein bild, 7, 11, 23, 25, 31, 44;
Library of Congress: cover, 13, 55, 56; Newscom: akg-images, 5, 41, 43, Album, 57
(bottom), Album/OLYMPIA-FILM, 38, dpa/picture-alliance/DB Walter Frentz Archive,
35, dpa/picture-alliance/Friedrich Rohrmann, 9, dpa/picture-alliance/Iopp-pool, 53;
Wikimedia: U.S. Army Signal Corps, 34

Library of Congress Cataloging-in-Publication Data
Cataloging-in-publication information is on file with the Library of Congress.
ISBN 978-0-7565-5528-3 (library binding)
ISBN 978-0-7565-5532-0 (paperback)
ISBN 978-0-7565-5544-3 (ebook pdf)

Printed in the United State of America.
10018S17

TABLEOFCONTENTS

ChapterOne
A GOLDEN MOMENT

As more than 100,000 buzzing spectators looked on, Jesse Owens stared at a pit of sand more than 100 feet (30.5 meters) away. On a humid August day in Berlin's Olympic Stadium, Owens was preparing for his second-to-last attempt in the long jump. Owens was already the world record holder in the event, but now he was competing for the United States in the 1936 Summer Olympics. While the mostly German crowd appreciated his athletic skills, many wanted Owens to lose. The man chasing Owens for the gold medal was one of their own—Luz Long.

Owens had won a gold medal the day before, in the 100-meter dash, and he was favored in the 200-meter run. But the long jump—also called the broad jump—was perhaps his best event, in which he combined his blazing speed with strength and perfect timing. No one had come close to beating his record jump of the year before—26 feet 8¼ inches.

In an earlier attempt that afternoon, Owens had taken the lead with a jump of 25 feet 10 inches, setting an Olympic record. Long had matched it. Now Owens had two more tries to regain the lead and win the gold.

One spectator watching the long-jump competition closely was German leader Adolf Hitler. His

Jesse Owens set an Olympic record in the long jump during the 1936 Berlin Games. His performance defied Adolf Hitler's racist beliefs.

government's anti-Semitic policies had prompted questions about whether the Berlin Games would go on and which countries would compete. Hitler had come to power as the leader of the Nazi Party, which became Germany's only political party. Its philosophy, sometimes called Nazism, rested on the theory that Germans were superior to all other people. Hitler particularly praised Germans who belonged to what he called the Aryan race. In Nazi thinking, the Aryans were the original settlers of Germany and northern Europe. They were warriors who supposedly conquered parts of Asia before moving westward. To Hitler, the Aryans were a "master race" that had a right to rule over what he and his followers considered the inferior peoples around them.

One of Hitler's goals was to keep Aryan blood "pure" and not allow "inferior" people to marry or have children with Germans. For the Nazis, the biggest threat to racial purity was the country's Jews. Hitler and his supporters blamed the Jews for most of Germany's problems since World War I. People with roots in Africa, such as the African-American Jesse Owens and his black teammates, were also considered inferior. During the games, Hitler bristled when someone suggested he have his picture taken with Owens. "I myself would never shake hands with one of them," the German dictator said.

Hitler had gained power using propaganda skillfully created and spread by Joseph Goebbels, one of his top aides. Goebbels shaped the Nazi message of

Adolf Hitler's personal photographer, Heinrich Hoffmann, photographed the Nazi leader (third from right) and German officials during the Berlin Games.

preserving the master race and uniting all Germans under Hitler. To make sure the people only saw and heard what Hitler and Goebbels wanted them to, the government tightly controlled what appeared in newspapers and was heard on the radio.

Hitler's attacks on Jews led some Americans and others to call for a boycott of the games. But supporters of the Berlin Games said the whole point of the Olympics was to improve understanding among the world's nations. The modern games began in 1896, thanks to the efforts of Baron Pierre de Coubertin of France. He was inspired by the ancient Olympics in Athens, Greece, thousands of years ago. If Greek cities were at war when the games began, the cities usually called a truce so their athletes could compete. Coubertin praised the value of sports for the world in a poem for the 1912 Olympic Games: "O Sport, you are Peace! You promote happy relations between peoples, bringing them together in their shared devotion to a strength which is controlled, organized and self-disciplined."

Hitler also believed in strength, particularly military strength. He had begun a huge effort to rebuild Germany's military, and he was planning to spread Nazi control beyond Germany. Hitler saw the Olympics as a way to both promote his country and deceive the world about his plans for war and domination.

Helping with this propaganda effort was actor and film director Leni Riefenstahl. The International Olympic Committee (IOC) chose her to film the Berlin Games and the Nazis paid for the project. Riefenstahl, who was not a member of the Nazi party, had made a famous documentary of a 1934 Nazi rally in Nuremberg, Germany. The movie, *Triumph of the Will*, used images of Hitler, the huge crowds, and the event's pageantry to promote the message of Hitler's power and the Nazis' supposed greatness. It is still considered one of the best examples of propaganda on film.

Leni Riefenstahl gave stage directions during the filming of her famous film *Triumph of the Will.*

For the Olympics, Riefenstahl demanded that she have complete artistic control over what she filmed. Joseph Goebbels resisted, but Hitler liked the director and granted her demand. Goebbels agreed with Riefenstahl that the movie should not focus only on German athletes and their triumphs. He realized that people would consider such a film to be simply propaganda and would dismiss it. Instead, Goebbels wanted a more balanced view of the games with coverage of foreign athletes, although not necessarily black athletes. For Riefenstahl, that included filming the black American athletes that Hitler and Goebbels despised. And the most famous African-American competing in Berlin was Jesse Owens. So, as Owens tried to win a gold medal in the long jump, Riefenstahl's camera crew filmed him in action.

The finals of the long jump pitted Owens against an athlete many considered the Nazis' perfect example of the ideal Aryan. Luz Long was tall, blue-eyed, blond, and strong. Owens later wrote that even he had admired Long's "perfectly proportioned body," its muscles shaped by "tens of thousands

Luz Long attempted to out-distance Jesse Owens in the long jump.

THE SNUB THAT DIDN'T HAPPEN?

Hitler publicly congratulated the German and Finnish winners of the shot put competition.

Jesse Owens was on the victory stand the day before his long-jump triumph to receive his gold medal in the 100-meter dash. One event of the 1936 Olympics that drew attention came right after he won that race. On the opening day of competition at the Berlin Games, Adolf Hitler had greeted victorious German and Finnish athletes, but he left the stadium without greeting two black American athletes who won medals in the high jump.

On the second day of competition, people watched to see how Hitler would react to Owens' success in the 100 meters. By then Olympic officials had told Hitler he could not ignore some athletes while praising others. He had to either meet with all the victors in public or none at all. Hitler chose to meet with none, though he still met with some favored Aryan athletes in a private spot in the stadium.

After the medal ceremony for the 100 meters, Owens walked toward Hitler's seat. What happened next was disputed by many who were there that day. One reporter said Hitler gave Owens "a friendly little Nazi salute." Another reporter said Hitler and Owens waved at each other. Owens claimed Hitler waved, though in later years he denied that it had happened. Some people in the stadium said they didn't see any wave, and some newspapers aimed at black readers in the United States said Hitler did not acknowledge Owens at all after his win. They said Hitler snubbed Owens because he was black. After the Olympics, Owens said the real snub came from his own president, Franklin D. Roosevelt. He told a crowd in Kansas City that "the president didn't even send me a telegram" to offer him congratulations.

of obvious hours of sweat and determination." Yet Owens had trained hard for years too, and his natural speed seemed to give him an advantage over the slower Long. The crowd had cheered wildly when Long tied Owens on his second jump. Now it watched as Owens began his second-to-last jump, hoping to take the lead again. He hit the board cleanly and leapt 26 feet 3¾ inches, once again setting an Olympic record.

Long had one more chance to tie or beat Owens, but after his sprint toward the pit, he jumped just past the board, meaning he had faulted and his jump didn't count. Long was finished, and Owens had won the gold medal. Owens, though, decided to make his last jump to see whether he could beat his own new record.

Grantland Rice, one of the great sportswriters of that era, described Owen's last leap: "As he hurled himself through space, [Owens] seemed to be jumping clear out of Germany. The American cheering started while Jesse was airborne." They could see that once again Owens was jumping a stunning distance. In an autobiography written years later, Owens described his thoughts and sensations as he jumped in Berlin: "I was reaching for the clouds … the clouds … the heavens."

On that last jump, Owens reached 26 feet 5½ inches—short of his world record, but well past what any Olympian had jumped before. And Owens had

"As he hurled himself through space, [Owens] seemed to be jumping clear out of Germany. The American cheering started while Jesse was airborne."

Heinrich Hoffmann photographed Jesse Owens flanked by the bronze and silver medal winners on the Olympic podium.

done it in front of the German leader, who considered Owens a member of an inferior race. Soon Owens, Long, and bronze-medal-winner Naoto Tajima of Japan went to the stand where the winning athletes were to receive their medals. Owens, with his gold, stood above the other two. Then, as "The Star Spangled Banner" played, Owens saluted the U.S. flag, his right hand to his forehead. Behind him, Long gave the stiff Nazi salute, his arm stretched forward. The photo that captured that moment became one of the most famous of the Berlin Games. It showed Owens' athletic success. But it also helped show how wrong Hitler was about African-Americans and all the others he thought beneath his master race.

Chapter Two

THE ROAD TO THE OLYMPICS

Jesse Owens' path to international athletic fame began in Cleveland, Ohio, where he first excelled in track-and-field competitions. But Owens began his life in rural Alabama. James Cleveland Owens was born in the town of Oakville on September 12, 1913. The grandson of former slaves, Owens was the youngest of 10 children. His father, Henry, was a sharecropper, raising cotton for a white land owner. He never learned to read, and in the segregated South of that era, Henry knew he would never be considered equal to whites. His wife, Emma, hoped for something better for her children than a life of poverty and fear of whites. In 1922 she persuaded her husband to move the family to Cleveland.

Jesse's family called him by his initials, J.C. When he entered elementary school in Cleveland, his teacher thought "J.C." was really "Jesse," and the new name stuck.

The family, even the children, found ways to make money, and while the Owenses were poor, they could afford to eat meat once a week—something they could never do in Alabama. Jesse delivered groceries and took other odd jobs to help out. He also liked to race the neighborhood kids, feeling a sense of freedom when he ran.

After junior high school, Owens would run track, and set many records, at East Technical High School.

When Owens was 13 and attending Fairmount Junior High School, a white man approached him. The man was Charles Riley, who taught physical education at Fairmount. He had seen Owens running and playing during recess and gym, and he thought that with proper training Owens could become an excellent runner. When Riley said he would help train him, Owens readily accepted the offer. He was eager to learn techniques that would give him an advantage over other runners. Riley later said Owens "yearned for every bit of instruction I could give him, and he

was always the last to quit practice in the evening."
One of Riley's instructions was to act as if he were
running on hot bricks and to let his feet barely touch
the ground. But Riley and Owens were not just a
teacher and student. They spent time together away
from the track, with Owens often eating Sunday
dinners with Riley and his family.

By the time Owens was 15, he was running the
100-yard dash in 11 seconds—an amazing speed
for someone his age. At Fairmount and then at East
Technical High School, he competed in that event as
well as the 220-yard dash, the long jump, and the low
hurdles. Owens wasn't the smoothest jumper over
the hurdles, but his speed between them made up for
any time he lost.

In his junior year of high school, Owens ran in a
100-meter race, slightly longer than the 100 yards he
usually ran, and seemed to have set a world record.
But his time did not become a record because track
officials ruled that the wind blowing from behind him
was too strong. They thought the wind gave Owens
an unfair advantage. Still, at 18, Owens had shown
he had the skills to be an international track star.
He proved it again later that summer at an event at
Cleveland's Municipal Stadium. A crowd of more than
50,000 came to see the competition, a sign of both the
interest in Owens, who by then had become a local
running sensation, and the general popularity of

Owens ran his way to U.S. track records while in high school.

track and field. At the event, Owens beat two Olympic medal winners. The next year, 1933, Owens tied the world record in the 100-yard dash and set national high school records in the 220 and the long jump.

Owens entered Ohio State University in the fall of 1933. As he had with Riley, Owens developed a good relationship with his new coach, Larry Snyder. First-year students at that time were not allowed to compete in varsity sports, so Owens' college career began the next year.

Owens became the first African-American captain of a Big Ten conference sports team when he was

Owens worked at a gas station to earn money during his college years.

elected captain of the OSU track team, but he still faced discrimination. He was not allowed to live in a campus dorm because he was black. He and other African-Americans were refused service at local restaurants. Traveling with the team to other colleges, Owens and his black teammates were sometimes turned away from restaurants that refused to serve African-Americans. Owens tried to not let the racism affect him. As his 1936 Olympic teammate Louis Zamperini later said, "[N]othing bothered him.

> "[N]othing bothered him. Somebody made a racial slur against him, and he'd say 'That's his problem, not mine.' So Jesse was great for returning, you might say, good for evil."

Somebody made a racial slur against him, and he'd say 'That's his problem, not mine.' So Jesse was great for returning, you might say, good for evil."

In May 1935 Owens, by then known as the Buckeye Bullet, had perhaps the greatest single day ever for a college athlete. Owens and his fellow Ohio State Buckeyes traveled to Michigan for the Big Ten track-and-field championships. For a time it looked as if Owens might not be able to compete. About a week before the championships, he was fooling around with a friend and fell down some stairs, hurting his back. In the days that followed, the pain moved into one of his legs. The day before the main events of the championships, Owens soaked in a hot tub, hoping the pain would go away. It didn't, but he competed anyway.

Owens competed first in the 100-yard dash on May 25 and tied the world record he already shared with Frank Wykoff, an Olympic gold-medal winner. "Jesse, that was phenomenal," said his coach, Larry Snyder. "I don't know how you did it." Despite the great time of 9.4 seconds, Owens was not satisfied. "I could have gone faster," said Owens. "I'm not bragging, but I really did get a bad start. Frankly, I am a little disappointed." Owens was known to be a little slow at the start sometimes, but he made up for it after running about 30 yards, where his superior speed usually helped propel him past the other sprinters.

The next event for Owens was the long jump. Before making his only jump of the day, he put a piece of paper at the 26-foot mark, so he'd have something to aim for. Owens sailed past the mark and set a world record of 26 feet 8¼ inches. A man standing by the jumping pit told Owens' coach that Owens had flown past him in the air at the height of the man's head—and the observer was 5 foot 8 inches (173 centimeters). "I wasn't surprised," Snyder said. "You have to get up that high if you are going to jump six inches better than the world's record." The Associated Press, which reported on the championships for newspapers around the country, said the "astonishing leap" set Owens "off in a class by himself as the all-time greatest broad jumper."

Next up for Owens was the 220-yard dash. Some sports experts thought he was even better at this event than the 100 because of the way he gained speed as he ran. That afternoon in Ann Arbor, Michigan, he won with a time of 20.3 seconds— another world record. The time was also faster than the world record for the 200 meters, which is almost the same distance as the 220. Then Owens ran his last race of the day, the 220-yard hurdles. The fans had already seen Owens make history—no track-and-field athlete had ever set world records in two different events on the same day. As Owens prepared for the 220, the crowd fell silent, waiting to see whether he could set another record. Owens did not disappoint—

he ran the event in 22.6 seconds, almost half a second faster than the old world record.

That historic day in Michigan made Owens a national sports hero. Newspapers aimed at black readers in particular held him up as a great example of what African-Americans could achieve when they did not face the barriers of racism and segregation. With the 1936 Berlin Olympics about one year away, many Americans figured Owens would be a star of the games. Still, he had competition from other good U.S. runners. He would have to excel in his events at the U.S. Olympic Trials in July 1936 to be sure of making the team. But some people wondered whether any American athletes would compete in the 1936 Games.

The International Olympic Committee had chosen Berlin as the site of the 1936 Games in 1931—almost two years before Adolf Hitler came to power. At first Hitler disliked the idea of hosting the games. Previously the Nazis had not wanted Germans to compete with athletes from the nations that had defeated Germany in World War I—which included the United States. With its loss in that war, Germany had to give up land and shrink its military to almost nothing. Hitler was determined to rebuild the military and take control of European lands where Germans lived and then conquer territory beyond that.

Hitler's attitude about the Olympics changed after he became Germany's leader. He came to believe that hosting them was "a splendid chance of enhancing our prestige abroad." Germany would show the world how the Nazis were creating a strong, modern nation, and the games would give Hitler a chance to show off the athletic talents of his supposedly superior Aryans. Despite holding complete power, the Nazis still did not have the support of many Germans. Hitler hoped the splendor of the Olympics would also help persuade more Germans to support the Nazi cause.

The Nazis spent several million dollars building a new stadium and other facilities for the Olympics. They wanted to match, if not surpass, the success of the 1932 Games, which had been held in Los Angeles, California. At the Berlin Games, Nazi officials did everything they could to impress visitors. Translators

Hitler hoped the splendor of the Olympics would also help persuade more Germans to support the Nazi cause.

Participants prepared to fly the Olympic flag after the conclusion of the first-ever torch run.

helped guests who did not speak German, and police pulled known thieves off the city's streets. The Nazis also added something new to the games—the carrying of a torch from the Olympics' ancient home in Greece to the Berlin stadium. More than 3,000 runners passed the torch to each other along the route. Film crews working for Leni Riefenstahl recorded some of the runners for her movie *Olympia*.

The torch run and the Olympics themselves almost didn't happen because of Hitler's ideas about race. He saw Europe's Jews as a distinct, inferior race, one that had tried to control Germany. He was clear about his goal to deny German Jews their rights and then remove them from the country altogether. Eventually his hateful ideas would grow, as he ordered the slaughter of Jews across Europe. That "Final Solution," known today as the Holocaust, was still to come. But from the beginning of Nazi rule, Hitler's party denied Jews their legal rights. That included kicking Jewish athletes off of Germany's national sports teams.

Nazi policies against the Jews grew stricter with the Nuremberg Laws of 1935. The laws defined who was Jewish based on whether their grandparents were Jews, not on whether they practiced the Jewish religion. German Jews had to carry identification cards that labeled them as Jews. They could not marry Germans, and the Nazis made clear their goal of further limiting the Jews' rights.

Well before the Nuremberg Laws, in April 1933, some American Jews and others who opposed Nazism called for a boycott of the Berlin Olympics. In the United States, supporters of a boycott turned to Avery Brundage. He was in charge of the American Olympic Committee, which supervised the participation of U.S. athletes in the games. Brundage opposed the boycott. He believed politics should be kept out of the Olympics. Of course, the Nazis had already introduced politics by keeping its Jewish athletes off its sports teams and seeking to use the

THE WINTER GAMES

Hitler gave the Nazi salute during opening ceremonies of the 1936 Winter Olympics.

Months before the Berlin Games, Germany also hosted the Winter Olympics of 1936. They were held in Bavaria, a region of Germany that was strongly anti-Semitic. Count Henri de Baillet-Latour, the Belgian president of the International Olympic Committee, visited the host villages of Garmisch and Partenkirchen and was shocked to see anti-Jewish slogans on signs. He told Adolf Hitler to have the signs removed before the Winter Games—and said that if he did not, the Berlin Games would be canceled.

Hitler had the anti-Semitic signs and posters temporarily removed. His critics realized that the Germans only wanted to make sure the games went on.

The Germans were not about to change their policies toward the Jews. Frederick T. Birchall of *The New York Times* reported that the Winter Games, on the whole, are "not being used for any active propaganda." He said, "However, this is really the most efficient propaganda conceivable. There is probably no tourist here who will not go home averring that Germany is the most peace-loving, unmilitaristic, hospitable and tolerant country in Europe and that all the foreign correspondents stationed here [reporting on Nazi racist policies] are liars." That, of course, was what Adolf Hitler and Joseph Goebbels hoped visitors would think for both the Winter and Summer Games.

games for propaganda. Still, Brundage resisted every effort to keep Americans out of the games or move the events to another country.

In the summer of 1934, Brundage visited Germany to see for himself what conditions were there. He returned to the United States and said the Nazis were treating Jewish athletes fairly. Critics of Hitler weren't convinced, and in 1935, George Messersmith, a U.S. diplomat who had spent time in Germany, said a boycott would show the Germans how much the world opposed the Nazis. The Germans, he said, were just "holding back on increased economic oppression against the Jews until the games are over." In the end, the Nazis let just one Jewish athlete compete for Germany in Berlin, fencer Helene Mayer. She was chosen not only for her skill, but also because she was only part Jewish. Joseph Goebbels accused white Americans who supported a boycott of ignoring the racism and discrimination in the United States against its black citizens.

After Brundage's trip, the American Olympic Committee voted to send a team to Berlin. But an organization called the Amateur Athletic Union (AAU) also tried to influence the matter. It oversaw amateur track-and-field events across the United States. Jeremiah Mahoney, president of the AAU, opposed Nazism and supported the idea of a boycott. The AAU, however, could not legally stop athletes from competing. All it could do was recommend that they boycott the games.

But Brundage opposed even a simple recommendation, fearing that some athletes would refuse to go. In December 1935, he helped defeat an AAU resolution that, among other things, called on "athletes and all those who love fair play to give no support or encouragement to the formation of an American team." The resolution was aimed at both the athletes and Americans who might donate money to a U.S. team. With the defeat of the resolution, the Germans could breathe more easily, since other nations were apt to follow what the Americans did.

Some African-Americans supported the idea of a U.S. boycott. They saw that Hitler's views on race applied to them as well. In August 1935, a leading black newspaper, the *New York Amsterdam News*, called on Jesse Owens and other black athletes to support the boycott. That November, the National Association for the Advancement of Colored People (NAACP) issued a similar statement. Some of its members, though, saw the disadvantage of a U.S. boycott. They realized that if Owens and other African-Americans excelled during the Olympics, their achievements would weaken Hitler's argument about inferior races.

Owens made a public statement about the proposed boycott. He wanted to compete, he said, but "if there are minorities in Germany who are being discriminated against, the United States should withdraw from the 1936 Olympics." Hearing about what Owens said, coach Larry Snyder tried to change his mind. He stressed that Owens was at the top of his game and had a great opportunity to win medals. Owens soon told the press that he was against the boycott after all.

For Owens to ensure that he would be going to Berlin, he had to do well at the U.S. Olympic Trials. Also competing for spots on the track-and-field team were several of Owens' top rivals and a runner named Mack Robinson. Mack's brother Jackie would

Shortly before heading to the U.S. Olympic Trials, Owens won four events at the 1936 National Collegiate Athletic Association (NCAA) track and field championships.

win fame in the battle against segregation in 1947, when he became the first African-American to play major league baseball.

At the trials, Owens won all three events he entered—the 100- and 200-meter runs and the broad jump. When he reached Berlin, the Germans treated him like a hero. They seemed to ignore Hitler's views on race, at least when it came to a track superstar like Owens. People gathered around him to take his picture, and in the stadium, they chanted his name. His gold-medal run in the 100 meters confirmed his status. Then came his duel with Luz Long.

ChapterThree
CAPTURING THE GAMES ON FILM

To Jesse Owens and other U.S. athletes, Carl-Ludwig "Luz" Long was something of a mystery. He had not competed in the United States, but he had won acclaim just before the Olympics when he set the European record in the long jump. Still, that leap was more than a foot shy of Owens' world record.

To reach the final rounds of the long jump, Owens and the other athletes had to qualify by jumping at least 23 feet 5 $\frac{13}{25}$ inches. For Owens, the Buckeye Bullet, that distance seemed a cinch. He'd been regularly beating that mark since high school. Before his first jump, Owens ran down the track and through the sand pit, a standard warm-up for the American jumpers. To his amazement, though, the judge signaled a foul. Owens learned that in the Olympics practice runs weren't allowed, so that counted as one of his three jumps to qualify.

The foul rattled Owens. He thought about being so far from home while Long had the advantage of competing close to his home, with fellow Germans cheering him on. Owens' stomach felt upset, and he had to silently shout to himself, "Stop thinking those thoughts!" As he prepared for his second jump, Owens tried to ignore Long and his own doubts and just make a jump he had made hundreds of times before. But his

jump was too short. Long, however, had easily beaten the qualifying distance and had made it into the finals.

On his last jump, Owens made sure he took off before reaching the board at the end of the runway, and he launched himself farther than he had the last time. He did not foul, and he cleared more than 25 feet. He was in the finals.

That set up the showdown with Long that the German fans had hoped for. Some Nazis had called the games "the Battle of the Colors"—white versus black. The U.S. team included 18 African-Americans, most of whom were competing in track-and-field events. The focus on race, at least among the Nazi leaders, showed in Joseph Goebbels' diaries. He wrote after the second day of the Olympics, "We Germans won a gold medal, the Americans three, of which two were Negroes. That is a disgrace. White people should be ashamed of themselves."

Long did not have the same concern about race. He just wanted to do his best for himself and his country. In the final round, after he made the jump that tied him with Owens for the lead, he soaked in the cheers from the German crowd. Then he looked over to the box where Hitler and other top Nazis sat. He saw the Führer (German for "great leader") joining in the applause. Long noted Hitler's "benevolent, fatherly smile."

But Hitler's smile would soon vanish, because with his last jump, Owens set an Olympic record. Showing his sportsmanship, Long rushed over to Owens and hugged him, happy for his record-setting leap. Long wrote soon after the games that "I couldn't help myself. I ran up to him, and I was the first to embrace and congratulate him. He responded by saying: 'You forced me to give my best!'" Then the two athletes walked arm and arm around the stadium track. As they waited for the awards ceremony, Owens and Long stretched out together on the grassy infield. Long later learned how upset Nazi officials had been about his friendly gestures toward Owens. He was told to never hug a black person again.

Luz Long and Jesse Owens relaxed as they waited for the medal ceremony.

Finally the time came to honor the winning athletes. Standing by the victory podium was photographer Heinrich Hoffmann, who took a photo that showed the proud, patriotic Owens saluting the Stars and Stripes as Long gave the Nazi salute. Ironically, the picture that disproved Hitler's beliefs on race was taken by someone who had helped spread Hitler's fame in Germany. Long before the Nazis rose to power, Hoffmann was already a well-known photographer in Germany. He took formal portraits and was also an early photojournalist, taking pictures of news events as they happened.

Hoffmann first saw Hitler at a 1920 rally in Munich. Hitler was delivering a political speech, but Hoffmann thought he was too unimportant to photograph. Hoffmann considered himself an artist and was not very interested in politics. Still, he joined the Nazi Party in April 1920. He took his first picture of Hitler three years later, after the two had become friends. Hoffmann and Hitler shared a love of art, and Hoffmann enjoyed what he called Hitler's "charming manners … [and] his happy enjoyment of the simple pleasures."

The relationship between Hitler and the photographer would last for more than 20 years, with Hoffmann taking more than 2 million photos of Hitler and the Nazis. Hoffmann's work became part of the propaganda meant to draw in Germans to the Nazi Party and show Germany's growing strength after Hitler took power. Hoffmann's work for the Nazis also made him rich. He sold some photos to newspapers, and Germans bought prints and books of his work. He probably never imagined that one of his most famous photos would become the one of Owens at the Berlin Games.

Aside from Hoffmann, the artist who perhaps most shaped Hitler's image in and outside of Germany was film director Leni Riefenstahl. While a photo can capture an important moment, a film

Heinrich Hoffmann's loyalty to Hitler would make him rich.

can tell a story that unfolds over time. Skillful filmmakers like Riefenstahl can edit footage to create the impressions they want. At the Berlin Games, Riefenstahl and her camera crews shot 1.4 million feet (427,000 m) of film, which Riefenstahl edited into a two-part movie called *Olympia*. The film was released almost two years after the games, and shorter versions of the film were produced for various countries.

Riefenstahl had been an actor before stepping behind the camera. During the 1920s she appeared in several German movies set in the Alps, called "mountain films." The natural settings and the strength the actors needed to ski and climb the peaks made the films distinct. Most German movies of the time were shot indoors. The rigorous filming led reviewers to call Riefenstahl a "sports actress."

Riefenstahl then directed her own mountain film, *Das Blaue Licht* (*The Blue Light*). It suggested that the German people should turn away from the modern world and embrace the outdoors, loyalty, and their ties to their country. Adolf Hitler tremendously enjoyed *Das Blaue Licht* when he saw it in 1932. Among other things, it matched the Nazi desire to champion simple Germans who were close to nature and worked with their hands. Germany, Hitler believed, had come to accept harmful, modern, foreign ideas that weakened its people. After Riefenstahl won acclaim for *Olympia, Das Blaue Licht* was released again in Germany. The Nazis praised it as "the most German of all films."

Riefenstahl wrote Hitler after she first heard him speak in 1932. The two soon met and developed a close relationship based on their love of movies. Almost immediately Hitler asked her to make films for the Nazis if they came to power. And after the success of *Triumph of the Will*, he was willing to give Riefenstahl almost anything she wanted to make *Olympia*. With the money she received, Riefenstahl made a documentary that went far beyond how newsreels of the day covered sports. Cameramen with telephoto lenses produced close-ups of the

Germany, Hitler believed, had come to accept harmful, modern, foreign ideas that weakened its people.

athletes' bodies and faces. Cameras sat on huge steel towers erected in the stadium to give a bird's-eye view. A member of Riefenstahl's staff invented a camera that could film swimming and diving events underwater. Riefenstahl dug a trench next to the jumping pit, so her cameras could sit below Jesse Owens and the other jumpers as they were in the air. When her cameras missed a winning performance, she had the athletes run or jump again just for her. Owens' record-setting jump was one of the events Riefenstahl re-created for her cameras.

For Riefenstahl, *Olympia* would be a piece of
art. She didn't want to simply record the events.
She wanted to show the human effort that went
into athletics, and the beauty of the competitors'
bodies. Instead of interviewing the athletes, she had
a narrator describe events, often with music playing
in the background. Slow-motion cameras, used for
the first time in recording sports events, added to the
artful effect Riefenstahl wanted. The true art, she
later said, came in editing the film. She had to decide

which scenes to include and how long they should last. "It is like composing music," she said. Seeing the images, she grew excited as the sporting action unfolded in front of her.

In keeping with Goebbels' aims, Riefenstahl did not make *Olympia* pure propaganda for the Nazis. That was clear in her footage of the long-jump competition between Owens and Long. But by including the event and others involving black Americans, she defied Goebbels. He had not wanted her to show them at all. But Riefenstahl kept Owens in, and the long jump became a highlight of the first part of *Olympia*. Her positive treatment of him led Germans to create a little rhyme: "Leni shows the Führer too / all that German film can do / He saw in negative print / how positive the Negro could sprint."

The day after Owens' record-setting long jump, he raced in the 200-meter finals. The race took place on a curved part of the stadium track, not on a straightaway. Owens' time of 20.7 seconds won him another gold medal and set a record for the event on a curved track.

Most Americans probably assumed the Olympics were then over for Owens. Newspapers reported that he would not be one of the runners in the 400-meter relay. For that event, each athlete carries a baton for 100 meters, then passes the baton to the next runner on his team. As *The New York Times* reported August 5, "Lawson Robertson, track coach, feels the

Ohio State Negro has done just about enough in one Olympics." At that time, the paper said, Robertson wasn't sure who his four runners would be, but the likely candidates were Marty Glickman, Sam Stoller, Foy Draper, and Frank Wykoff.

To the surprise of many, when it came time for the 400-meter relay, Owens was on the track. Robertson had chosen him and another fast African-American sprinter, Ralph Metcalfe. Hearing that Glickman and Stoller were out, Owens supposedly said, "I've already got three gold medals, I don't need any more." But over the previous few days, he had also told reporters he wouldn't mind a shot at a fourth medal. And he and his teammates did win the gold. As the largest crowd of the Olympics watched Owens' last performance of the games, the Americans won with a world-record time of 39.8 seconds.

Many people had called the Berlin Olympics the "Nazi Games." And the Germans had done well, winning the most medals and the most gold medals. The United States placed second in each category. But Marty Glickman saw it differently. Years later, he said, "I saw that they were Jesse Owens Olympic Games. The myth of Nazi Aryan supremacy was smashed to smithereens by the great non-Aryan athletes."

WAS IT PREJUDICE?

The 400-meter relay team—Owens (from left), Ralph Metcalfe, Foy Draper, and Frank Wykoff

Questions have been raised since 1936 about why Marty Glickman and Sam Stoller, the U.S. team's only Jewish members, were dropped from the 400-meter relay race. One theory was that the track team's assistant coach, Dean Cromwell, wanted to make sure runners from his school competed. Cromwell coached at the University of Southern California and Foy Draper and Frank Wykoff had gone there. Draper had lost to Stoller and Glickman in time trials the week before.

A reporter wrote at the time that Coach Lawson Robertson feared that the Germans and the Dutch had secretly found runners who were turning in surprisingly fast times, and he wanted his best sprinters on the track. Owens and Metcalfe were the fastest at 100 meters. When Robertson expressed his theory about the

secret runners, Glickman said, in disbelief, "Coach, you can't hide world-class sprinters."

Glickman and Wykoff believed there was prejudice at work—prejudice against the track team's only two Jewish members. Glickman thought that coaches Robertson and Cromwell and Olympic official Avery Brundage were all anti-Semitic. He thought team officials did not want to have two American Jewish athletes on the victory stand, because of the Nazi attitude toward the Jews. Years later he said he had learned that the Nazis had pressured the Americans to remove Stoller and him. Stoller did not publicly talk about anti-Semitism, but he told reporters, "I do not think I was treated fairly."

ChapterFour
POLITICS AND THE OLYMPICS

Heinrich Hoffmann's picture of Jesse Owens was not the only famous photo of the athlete from the 1936 Berlin Games. One image shows Long and Owens relaxing together on the Olympic Stadium field. Another shows Owens leaving the starting line on his gold-medal run in the 100 meters. But today when people want to show how Jesse Owens contradicted Adolf Hitler's ideas about race, Hoffmann's picture is often used. After Germany invaded Poland in 1939, setting off World War II in Europe, the photo's impact seemed to grow. Hitler's early military successes let him start his efforts to wipe out Europe's Jews and others he considered inferior. Hitler and his Nazis slaughtered more than 11 million people, including 6 million Jews, during what came to be called the Holocaust. Many more would have died if the United States, Great Britain, the Soviet Union, and their allies had not united to defeat Germany.

Soon after the Berlin Games, Hitler showed that he had no respect for the Olympic value of world peace. He gave orders for the country to increase its efforts to rebuild its military, to prepare for his future war aims. And Hitler said the Olympic Games would no longer take place in various countries. Germany, once it achieved military victory, would be the permanent site of the games.

Hungarian Jews sent to the Auschwitz concentration camp were among the 6 million Jews murdered by the Nazis during the Holocaust.

Hoffmann would never have a chance to photograph those future games. The war led to the cancellation of the 1940 and 1944 Olympics. After the war, Hoffmann was tried as a war criminal. The Allies accused him of making profits off the war, through the sales of his photos. He was found guilty and sentenced to 10 years in prison, although he only served about five years. After his release, he gave up photography, but he wrote his autobiography. He called it *Hitler Was My Friend*.

With his four gold medals, Jesse Owens was clearly the star of the Berlin Games. He tied what was then the individual record for most golds

in track-and-field events in a single Olympics. Before leaving Berlin, Owens considered turning professional, meaning he could accept money for taking part in athletic and commercial events. Taking the money meant he would no longer be able to compete for Ohio State, but his coach, Larry Snyder, supported the move. "It would be foolish for me to stand in Jesse's way," Snyder said. "He's absolutely at the height of his fame now."

But in the meantime, Owens was still an amateur, and before returning to the United States, he and other U.S. Olympians were supposed to compete in events across Europe. The competitions were going to raise money for the Amateur Athletic Union. The promoters promised the AAU more money if Owens appeared than if he didn't, and the organization needed the money. Despite being tired from the Olympic Games and missing his family back in Ohio, Owens had to keep running and jumping. Finally, during the tour, Owens met with Snyder and officials from the NCAA.

The association supervises college sports in the United States. The officials thought the AAU was greedy, and they could see how much Owens wanted to go home. They also knew that once he got back to the States, Owens could start making money for himself, not the AAU. They told him he should go back to Cleveland, and Owens agreed.

The decision upset AAU officials, and they suspended Owens from any future amateur athletic events in the United States. Avery Brundage of the International Olympic Committee, who once ran the AAU, supported the decision. Owens, though, did not seem to mind. He was ready to turn professional and try to make money for himself and his family.

Owens learned, however, that many of the people who talked about offering him large contracts could not follow through. And despite his Olympic heroics, Owens and his family struggled to find a hotel room in New York City, where they gathered when Owens got back from Europe. The owners of some of the

city's finest hotels turned the Owenses away because of the owners' prejudice against black people. There and in Ohio, Owens received parades in his honor, but he realized he was not going to cash in on his fame, as he had hoped. And even though he had not received money for sports, the AAU stuck to its guns and said he could not compete in any future amateur events. A frustrated Owens said, "I'm getting good and tired of getting kicked around."

"I'm getting good and tired of getting kicked around."

Owens did get paid for some public appearances he made through the end of 1936. One of the events was a race against a horse in Havana, Cuba. Given a head start, Owens beat the horse and its jockey and earned $2,000. Years later, Owens said he had been embarrassed to make money that way. But at the time, he said he would gladly race another horse again, even without the head start. And he did.

Over the next several years, Owens took several jobs to try to support his family. He invested in a dry-cleaning business, worked briefly for the Ford Motor Company, and took a job with the state of Illinois, supervising sporting events. He also appeared at sporting events, being paid to greet fans.

During the 1950s, Owens helped the U.S. government. The United States was involved in the Cold War with the Soviet Union. The two countries were trying to spread their influence and political values around the world. The Soviet Union had a communist government, with a single party controlling the government and the economy. That system is at odds with capitalism, the economic system of the United States, which is based on the freedom to own property. Owens traveled to foreign nations to talk about the opportunities African-Americans had under capitalism and democracy. He represented U.S. President Dwight D. Eisenhower at the 1956 Summer Games in Melbourne, Australia, and he continued

President Gerald Ford presented Owens with the Presidential Medal of Freedom at a White House ceremony.

to represent his country around the world for years to come. In 1976 President Gerald Ford gave Owens the Presidential Medal of Freedom, the highest government honor a U.S. civilian can receive.

In the years after the 1936 Olympics, Jesse Owens continued to talk about his relationship with Luz Long. He said the two wrote each other letters even after Long joined the German army. Long died in 1943 from war wounds suffered fighting against the Americans and their allies. According to Owens, their friendship began right before the long-jump event at the Berlin Games. As the story goes, Long helped steady Owens' nerves during the qualifying jumps. He even put down a towel to mark where Owens should begin his jump. From then on, the two competitors were the unlikely pair—a German Aryan and a black American—who defied Hitler. Owens told this story many times until his death in 1980.

In recent years, however, some people began to wonder whether all of Owens' details about his relationship with Long were accurate. In 2009 U.S. athletes competed at an international track event in Berlin for the first time since 1936. The news media looked back at the Long-Owens friendship, and National Public Radio reported that the story was partly a myth.

It said Olympic historian Tom Ecker and a colleague had asked Owens about the long jump. Ecker said, "Jesse Owens admitted to us that he had not met Luz Long until after the competition was over." Owens suggested another time that he told stories that "people like to hear." The story of his friendship with Long certainly impressed people. In 2012 the German newsmagazine *Der Spiegel* also suggested that Owens' version of events might not be right. Referring to material about Long's life that his son Kai had collected, including letters, diary entries, and newspaper articles, the magazine said none of it provided "any evidence to support Owens' claims of his wonderful friendship with Long."

What was true, however, was that Long embraced Owens after his last jump, and the two walked arm in arm around the track. And no one could deny the ease they seemed to share in the photos of them lounging next to each other in the stadium. Whatever relationship Owens and Long had in Berlin and after, it endured through Long's son Kai. In 1951, Owens traveled to Germany with the Harlem Globetrotters basketball team. In Hamburg, the younger Long and Owens met for the first time. They met again 13 years later, when Owens made the movie *Jesse Owens Returns to Berlin*. The Long and Owens families shared a connection that lasted after Owens' death in 1980. At the 2009 Berlin track event, Kai Long and his daughter met with Marlene Dortch, Owens' granddaughter. Together the relatives of the stars of the 1936 long jump awarded the medals to the winners of the 2009 competition.

The story of their friendship remains famous today. The reputation of Leni Riefenstahl's *Olympia*, which has been called a masterpiece, has also held up over the decades. Film fans admire its technical brilliance and Riefenstahl's ability to make sports seem so beautiful. During the 1960s, a New York show featured German films made from 1908 to 1958. The program notes said some film experts considered *Olympia* "one of the most splendid motion pictures produced in any era, in any country." The program noted that Riefenstahl did not try to "understate the achievements of the Negro athletes led by the remarkable performance of Jesse Owens."

A street in front of Berlin's Olympic Stadium is named after Owens.

Owens appreciated how Riefenstahl portrayed him in the film. In 1972, the Summer Olympics were in Munich, Germany. They were the first German Games since 1936. Owens and the filmmaker both attended an event in Munich. When they saw each other, Riefenstahl later wrote, "it was a deeply emotional meeting. ... [W]e were both near to tears." Owens told the crowd that there was a "lady here who is important in my life." He then began to clap, to encourage Riefenstahl to stand and be recognized. Slowly, the crowd began to clap and cheer, and Riefenstahl came up to Owens and thanked him.

The people in the crowd that day were not sure how to react to Owens' praise. For many, Riefenstahl was then seen as just a propaganda filmmaker for Hitler. Riefenstahl had not helped herself by denying that she ever had been close to Hitler and the Nazis. She claimed for decades that the Nazis had not paid for *Olympia*, though historians found documents proving that they did.

Toward the end of Riefenstahl's life, some film experts tried to take a more balanced view of her work. She clearly supported the Nazis, and her films helped their cause. As biographer Jürgen Trimborn wrote in 2002, a year before Riefenstahl's death, "she must have been aware that [*Olympia*] enhanced the prestige" of Nazi Germany. Yet no one could deny that she had created great films. She remained, as many newspapers noted after her death, a controversial figure in 20th century art.

Hitler's use of the Berlin Games for his own purposes showed how hard it can be to keep politics and sports separate. In the decades after World War II, politics have entered the Olympics in various ways. During the Cold War, the Soviet Union tried to connect its athletes' success during the Olympics with the strength of its communist system. Soviet officials declared that their victories proved communism was better than capitalism.

Political conflicts away from the games have sometimes entered the competition. At the 1956

AN OLYMPIC PRESENCE

Avery Brundage is viewed as the International Olympic Committee's most controversial leader.

When Israeli athletes were murdered at the 1972 Olympics in Munich, a major figure from the Berlin Games was still an important Olympic figure. Avery Brundage became president of the International Olympic Committee in 1952 and held that position until after the Munich Games. Over the years he sometimes drew criticisms for his actions. In opposing the 1936 boycott, Brundage insisted that politics had no place in sports. But some people thought he simply did not want to embarrass Adolf Hitler and that he actually supported the Nazi government and anti-Semitism.

In writing against the boycott, Brundage blamed communists for stirring up the anti-German feelings and said "certain Jews had better understand that they cannot use these Games as a weapon in their boycott against the Nazis." Hitler often accused communists and Jews of being the source of Germany's troubles, and Brundage seemed to see them playing a disruptive role in the United States. Brundage was also accused of playing a part in the removal of the two Jewish runners from the American 400-meter relay team. Two years after the games, a construction company Brundage owned was chosen to help build the German Embassy in Washington, D.C., which showed his close relations with Nazi officials. (It was not built because of World War II.)

After the Munich massacre in 1972, Brundage insisted that the games had to go on. He seemed to equate the killing of the Israelis with peaceful protests before the games in favor of excluding Rhodesia. The African nation—now known as Zimbabwe—had a white government that denied the political rights of black people. Rhodesia was banned from the games, a move Brundage had opposed. His comments linking the Israelis' murders with the protests struck some people as extremely insensitive.

Summer Games in Melbourne, Australia, water polo players from the U.S.S.R. and Hungary battled each other in the pool. Before the games, Soviet troops had gone into Hungary to violently end a rebellion against communist rule. In the water polo match, a Soviet player threw a punch that drew a Hungarian's blood.

The worst case of violence at the Olympics came at the 1972 Summer Games in Munich. Palestinian terrorists kidnapped 11 Israeli athletes, coaches, and officials. Many Palestinians, like Palestinians today, wanted to create their own independent nation in lands controlled by Israel. Conflict between the two sides has led to several wars. In Munich, the terrorist group Black September demanded the release of 234 prisoners, mostly Palestinians held in Israeli jails. The kidnappers eventually killed all the Israeli hostages and one German. Ever since then, people have tried to honor their memory. But the International Olympic Committee has not been receptive. It refused to authorize a moment of silence at the 2012 London Games. Finally, in 2016, the victims of the Munich terrorist attack were commemorated at the Summer Games in Brazil.

Just as politics led some Americans to call for a boycott of the 1936 Games, Cold War politics led to actual boycotts decades later. In 1980 the United States and some allies refused to compete at the Olympics in Moscow, the capital of the Soviet Union. President Jimmy Carter wanted to show his

anger over the Soviets' refusal to withdraw from Afghanistan, which they had invaded in 1979. In response, the Soviet Union and its allies boycotted the 1984 Summer Olympics in Los Angeles.

A boycott in 1936 would have deprived Jesse Owens of the chance to show his athletic talents to the world. He and the other black American athletes would not have been able to challenge Adolf Hitler's warped views on race. But Owens had his chance to shine, and a photograph and a film captured a positive moment in history that still touches people today.

Timeline

1913

James Cleveland Owens is born September 12 in Oakville, Alabama

1922

The Owens family moves to Cleveland, Ohio

1932

Owens apparently sets a record in the 100-meter run, but it does not count because of a high tail wind; he defeats two Olympic medal winners in a race in Cleveland

1933

Adolf Hitler and his Nazi Party win control of the German government; Owens sets national high school records in the long jump and the 220-yard dash; Owens enters Ohio State University in the fall

Owens sets his first track records under his first track coach, Charles Riley; he then stars in track and field at East Technical High School

1931

The International Olympic Committee awards Germany the 1936 Summer and Winter Olympics

1935

Leni Riefenstahl releases her propaganda film *Triumph of the Will*; Owens sets three world records and ties another in one day; Germany passes laws restricting the freedom of its Jewish population; Avery Brundage leads an effort to stop a boycott of the 1936 Summer Games

Timeline

1936

Owens wins four gold medals at the Berlin Olympics, which helped disprove Hitler's theories about a master race; Riefenstahl films the Berlin Games; Owens refuses to compete for the AAU in Europe and loses the right to compete as an amateur

1938

Riefenstahl releases *Olympia* to wide acclaim

1972

Members of the Palestinian terrorist group Black September kill 11 Israelis at the Munich Games; Owens and Riefenstahl meet in Munich

1951

Owens meets Kai Long, the son of his main competitor in the long jump at the Berlin Games

1939

German forces invade Poland, starting World War II

1947

Heinrich Hoffmann is tried and convicted of war profiteering

1980

Jesse Owens dies March 31; he was 66

Glossary

allies—people or nations that work together for a common cause

anti-Semitism—hostility to or prejudice against Jews

boycott—to refuse to take part in something as a protest

capitalism—economic system that allows people to freely create businesses and own as much property as they can afford

communism—system in which goods and property are owned by the government and shared in common; communist rulers limit personal freedoms to achieve their goals

discrimination—unfair treatment of a person or group

newsreels—short movies dealing with current events that were shown in movie theaters before the main film

oppression—an unjust or cruel exercise of authority or power

photojournalism—use of photography to capture events and persons in the news

prejudice—hatred or unfair treatment of people who belong to a certain social group

propaganda—information spread to try to influence the thinking of people; often not completely true or fair

resolution—formal expression of opinion, will, or intent voted on by an official body or assembled group

segregated—having separate schools and other public places for people based on their race

sharecropper—farmer who works land owned by someone else in exchange for housing and part of the profits

Additional Resources

Further Reading

Altman, Linda Jacobs. *Adolf Hitler and the Rise of the Third Reich*. New York: Enslow Publishing, 2016.

Nardo, Don. *Hitler in Paris: How a Photograph Shocked a World at War*. North Mankato, Minn.: Compass Point Books, 2014.

Stanmyre, Jackie F. *Jesse Owens: Facing Down Hitler*. New York: Cavendish Square, 2016.

Internet Sites

Use FactHound to find Internet sites related to this book. All of the sites on FactHound have been researched by our staff.

Here's all you do:
Visit *www.facthound.com*
Type in this code: 9780756555283

Critical Thinking Using the Common Core

Do you think American athletes should have boycotted the 1936 Berlin Games? Why or why not? (Integration of Knowledge and Ideas)

In discussing racism and discrimination, fellow Olympian Louis Zamperini said nothing bothered Jesse Owens. Do you think that is true? Why or why not? (Key Ideas and Details)

What were some of the techniques Leni Riefenstahl used to make *Olympia* unlike other films about sports? (Craft and Structure)

Source Notes

Page 6, line 24: Jeremy Schaap. *Triumph: The Untold Story of Jesse Owens and Hitler's Olympics*. Boston: Houghton Mifflin, 2007, p. 195.

Page 8, line 7: Pierre de Coubertin. "Ode to Sport." *Olympic Review*. April-May 2000, p. 29. 6 June 2016. http://library.la84.org/OlympicInformationCenter/OlympicReview/2000/OREXXVI32/OREXXVI32x.pdf

Page 10, line 9: Jesse Owens and Paul G. Neimark. *Jesse: A Spiritual Autobiography*. Plainfield, N.J.: Logos International, 1978, p. 62.

Page 11, col. 2, line 4: *Triumph: The Untold Story of Jesse Owens and Hitler's Olympics*, p. 192.

Page 11, col. 2, line 14: David Clay Large. *Nazi Games: The Olympics of 1936*. New York: W. W. Norton, 2007, p. 233.

Page 12, line 18: *Triumph: The Untold Story of Jesse Owens and Hitler's Olympics*, p. 207.

Page 12, line 25: *Jesse: A Spiritual Autobiography*, p. 76.

Page 15, line 10: Chris Brasher. "From the Vault: Jesse Owens in His Own Words." *The Guardian*. 31 March 2008. 7 June 2016. https://www.theguardian.com/sport/blog/2008/apr/01/fromthevaultjesseowensin

Page 18, line 10: "Jesse Owens." American Experience. PBS. 7 June 2016. http://www.pbs.org/wgbh/americanexperience/features/transcript/owens-transcript/

Page 19, line 20: Jeremy Schaap. "The Olympian and the Dictator." *Runner's World*. March 2007, pp. 77–78.

Page 20, line 9: Larry Snyder. "My Boy Jesse." *The Saturday Evening Post*. 7 Nov. 1936. 7 June 2016. http://www.saturdayeveningpost.com/2016/02/19/history/post-perspective/boy-jesse.html

Page 20, line 14: "Owens Surpasses Three World Records." *The New York Times*. 26 May 1935, p. S1.

Page 22, line 15: Piers Brendon. *The Dark Valley: A Panorama of the 1930s*. New York: Knopf, 2000, p. 521.

Page 25, col. 2, line 4: Frederick T. Birchall. "Crowded Program at the Games Keeps Garmisch Visitors on Jump." *The New York Times*. 12 Feb. 1936, p. 28.

Page 26, line 12: *Triumph: The Untold Story of Jesse Owens and Hitler's Olympics*, p. 71.

Page 27, line 23: "A.A.U. Blocks Vote on Olympics Ban; New Fight Today." *The New York Times*. 8 Dec. 1935, p. 1.

Page 28, line 16: "Jesse Owens." American Experience. 7 June 2016. http://www.pbs.org/wgbh/americanexperience/features/introduction/owens/

Page 30, line 22: *Jesse: A Spiritual Autobiography*, p. 63.

Page 32, line 3: "The Man Behind Hitler." American Experience. 7 June 2016. http://www.pbs.org/wgbh/amex/goebbels/peopleevents/e_olympics.html

Page 32, line 15: Michael Wulzinger. "Hitler's 'Battle of the Colors': Doubt Cast on Olympic Friendship between Owens and Long." *Spiegel* Online. 27 Jan. 2012. 8 June 2016. http://www.spiegel.de/international/zeitgeist/hitler-s-battle-of-the-colors-doubt-cast-on-olympic-friendship-between-owens-and-long-a-811582.html

Page 32, line 20: Ibid.

Page 34, line 12: Heinrich Hoffmann. *Hitler Was My Friend*. Translated by R. H. Stevens. London: Burke, 1955, p. 49.

Page 36, line 3: Jürgen Trimborn. *Leni Riefenstahl: A Life*. Translated by Edna McCown. New York: Faber and Faber, 2007, p. 31.

Page 36, line 17: Ibid., p. 55.

Page 39, line 2: Leni Riefenstahl. *A Memoir*. New York: St. Martin's Press, 1993, p. 205.

Page 39, line 14: *Nazi Games: The Olympics of 1936*, p. 307.

Page 39, line 29: "Owens Out of Relay." *The New York Times*. 5 Aug. 1936, p. 27.

Page 40, line 10: *Triumph: The Untold Story of Jesse Owens and Hitler's Olympics*, p. 223.

Page 40, line 23: Marty Glickman Interview. The Nazi Olympics: Berlin 1936. United States Holocaust Memorial Museum. 20 May 1996. 8 June 2016. http://collections.ushmm.org/oh_findingaids/RG-50.429.0004_trs_en.pdf

Page 41, col. 2, line 1: Ibid.

Page 41, col. 2, line 13: The Associated Press. "Stoller Declares He Will Quit Track." *The New York Times*. 10 Aug. 1936, p. 13.

Page 44, line 7: The Associated Press. "Owens to Turn Pro If Offers Suit Him." *The New York Times*. 11 Aug. 1936, p. 26.

Page 46, line 8: William J. Baker. *Jesse Owens: An American Life*. New York: The Free Press, 1986, p. 131.

Page 49, line 16: Tom Goldman. "Was Jesse Owens' 1936 Long-Jump Story a Myth?" NPR. 14 Aug. 2009. 9 Aug. 2016. http://www.npr.org/templates/story/story.php?storyId=111878822

Page 49, line 19: Ibid.

Page 49, line 26: "Hitler's 'Battle of the Colors': Doubt Cast on Olympic Friendship between Owens and Long."

Page 50, line 25: *A Memoir*, p. 527.

Page 50, line 27: Ibid.

Page 51, line 6: Ibid., p. 580.

Page 51, line 8: Frank Deford. "The Ghost of Berlin." *Sports Illustrated*. 4 Aug. 1986. 13 June 2016. http://www.si.com/vault/1986/08/04/113743/the-ghost-of-berlin-fifty-years-ago-leni-riefenstahl-directed-a-brilliant-film-about-the-olympics-but-her-association-with-adolf-hitler-has-shadowed-her-life

Page 52, line 13: *Leni Riefenstahl: A Life*, p. 152.

Page 53, col. 1, line 14: *Nazi Games: The Olympics of 1936*, p. 93.

Select Bibliography

"A.A.U. Blocks Vote on Olympics Ban; New Fight Today." *The New York Times*. 8 Dec. 1935, p. 1.

The Associated Press. "Owens to Turn Pro If Offers Suit Him." *The New York Times*. 11 Aug. 1936, p. 26.

The Associated Press. "Stoller Declares He Will Quit Track." *The New York Times*. 10 Aug. 1936, p. 13.

Baker, William J. *Jesse Owens: An American Life*. New York: The Free Press, 1986.

Birchall, Frederick T. "Crowded Program at the Games Keeps Garmisch Visitors on Jump." *The New York Times*. 12 Feb. 1936, p. 28.

Brasher, Chris. "From the Vault: Jesse Owens in His Own Words." *The Guardian*. 31 March 2008. 7 June 2016. https://www.theguardian.com/sport/blog/2008/apr/01/fromthevaultjesseowensin

Brendon, Piers. *The Dark Valley: A Panorama of the 1930s*. New York: Knopf, 2000.

Deford, Frank. "The Ghost of Berlin." *Sports Illustrated*. 4 Aug. 1986. 13 June 2016. http://www.si.com/vault/1986/08/04/113743/the-ghost-of-berlin-fifty-years-ago-leni-riefenstahl-directed-a-brilliant-film-about-the-olympics-but-her-association-with-adolf-hitler-has-shadowed-her-life

Goldman, Tom. "Was Jesse Owens' 1936 Long-Jump Story a Myth?" NPR. 14 Aug. 2009. 9 Aug. 2016. http://www.npr.org/templates/story/story.php?storyId=111878822

Hilton, Christopher. *How Hitler Hijacked World Sport: the World Cup, the Olympics, the Heavyweight Championship and the Grand Prix*. Charleston, S.C.: The History Press, 2011.

Hoffmann, Heinrich. *Hitler Was My Friend*. Translated by R. H. Stevens. London: Burke, 1955.

"Jesse Owens." American Experience. PBS. 7 June 2016. http://www.pbs.org/wgbh/americanexperience/features/transcript/owens-transcript/

Kershaw, Ian. *Hitler: A Biography*. New York: W. W. Norton, 2008.

Large, David Clay. *Nazi Games: The Olympics of 1936*. New York: W. W. Norton, 2007.

"The Man Behind Hitler." American Experience. 7 June 2016. http://www.pbs.org/wgbh/amex/goebbels/peopleevents/e_olympics.html

Marty Glickman Interview. The Nazi Olympics: Berlin 1936. United States Holocaust Memorial Museum. 20 May 1996. 8 June 2016. http://collections.ushmm.org/oh_findingaids/RG-50.429.0004_trs_en.pdf

Owens, Jesse, and Paul G. Neimark. *Jesse: A Spiritual Autobiography*. Plainfield, N.J.: Logos International, 1978.

"Owens Out of Relay." *The New York Times*. 5 Aug. 1936, p. 27.

"Owens Surpasses Three World Records." *The New York Times*. 26 May 1935, p. S1.

Riefenstahl, Leni. *A Memoir*. New York: St. Martin's Press, 1993.

Schaap, Jeremy. "The Olympian and the Dictator." *Runner's World*. March 2007, pp. 77–78.

Schaap, Jeremy. *Triumph: The Untold Story of Jesse Owens and Hitler's Olympics*. Boston: Houghton Mifflin, 2007.

Snyder, Larry. "My Boy Jesse." *The Saturday Evening Post*. 7 Nov. 1936. 7 June 2016. http://www.saturdayeveningpost.com/2016/02/19/history/post-perspective/boy-jesse.html

Trimborn, Jürgen. *Leni Riefenstahl: A Life*. Translated by Edna McCown. New York: Faber and Faner, 2007.

Wulzinger, Michael. "Hitler's 'Battle of the Colors': Doubt Cast on Olympic Friendship between Owens and Long." *Spiegel* Online. 27 Jan. 2012. 8 June 2016. http://www.spiegel.de/international/zeitgeist/hitler-s-battle-of-the-colors-doubt-cast-on-olympic-friendship-between-owens-and-long-a-811582.html

Index

About the Author

Michael Burgan has written many books for children and young adults during his 20 years as a freelance writer. Most of his books have focused on history. Burgan has won several awards for his writing. He lives in Santa Fe, New Mexico.